Searching for Jug Bay Sanctuary

Searching for Jug Bay Sanctuary

poems by Kathy Kramer-Howe

Haley's
Athol, Massachusetts

© 2025 by Kathy Kramer-Howe.

All rights reserved. With the exception of short excerpts in a review or critical article, no part of this book may be re-produced by any means, including information storage and retrieval or photocopying equipment, without written permission of the publisher, Haley's.

Haley's
488 South Main Street
Athol, MA 01331
haley.antique@verizon.net
978.249.9400

Photos by Kathy Kramer-Howe.
Cover photo courtesy of Kathy Kramer-Howe.
Copy edited by Mary-Ann DeVita Palmieri.

International Standard Book Number, paperback:
 978-1-956055-21-4
International Standard Book Number, ebook:
 978-1-956055-22-1

Library of Congress Control Number: 2025931427

for my beloved husband, Rick
loving each other the greatest spiritual adventure

for my sisters, Lynn and Sally
siblings through life and deeply a part of one another

Contents

Poems as Sanctuary in Ordinary Life
    an introduction by Kathy Kramer-Howe................1

Ordinary Days

Starbuck's Twenty- Gram Protein Box 5
The Kestrels Fledge 6
Trespassing as Fine Art 7
Hawks...8
Hot Latte, Sprinkle of Lavender...........................9
Bella Knew She Was Borrowed 10
Wake-Up Call... 12
A Colombian Woman 13
Cat Quincy's Magnificent Sniffer 14
In Front of the Meat Display 15
Everyday Miracles....................................... 16
For Success in Aging 17

Forgetfulness

Breezy Point, Maryland 21
Chesapeake Nightfall 22
At the Eye Doctor 23
A Shrine in Paradise, Prince Frederick 24
Saint Patrick's Day 25
Birthday Dinner... 26
Bearded Irises in North Beach 27
Empty Nest.. 28
Binary 29
Searching for Jug Bay Sanctuary 30
Harbor... 31

Other Places

Massachusetts in May 35
Not Raindrops 36
York Beach, Maine 37

Floating, Desolation Canyon, Utah 38
At the Tambo Hotel, Johannesburg 39
Feeling Mainos. 40
Punta Moreno Landing, Galápagos 41
Ocean Inside 42
Pine Woods Triptych, Flagstaff........................ 43
Two White-Tailed Deer Near an Abbey 44
We Made It From 45
Acknowledgements..................................... 47
About the Author..................................... 49
Colophon... 51

Poems as Sanctuary in Ordinary Life

an introduction by Kathy Kramer-Howe

Jug Bay Wetlands Sanctuary lies in Lothian, Anne Arundel County, Maryland. It protects about seventeen hundred acres of Patuxent River tidal reaches and wetlands, giving crucial refuge to animal and plant life. Pottery shards show evidence of human habitation going back eleven thousand years. Twice I have driven out to visit it, with its boardwalks across marshes and riverine beaches, without finding it. I hope to succeed someday and, meanwhile, poetry reminds me to keep searching.

As I assembled poems for *Searching for Jug Bay Sanctuary*, I came to see them as a sort of sanctuary in ordinary life. When I become present to what is around me, a felt response inside invites me to go deeper. Why did I care about a Vietnamese altar in a nail shop, a protein snack at a coffee bar, a neighborhood walk with a friend's dog? How did sitting with my sister in silence connect me suddenly to our early childhood?

Searching for Jug Bay Sanctuary includes three sections. "Ordinary Days" has poems that arrived during the most routine times: shopping, a stop at Starbucks, gazing out a window. "Forgetfulness" contains poems written in response to my older sister Lynn's sudden onset of dementia, which started in 2020 during the COVID pandemic. My younger sister Sally and I kept her safe, solvent, and cared for in her final years. The eldest of us three, she could genuinely be called a survivor—of alcohol and nicotine addiction, among other challenges. Yet she triumphed, loved her career as a registered nurse, and inspired many others to become nurses, too. Finally, highlighting how travel can wake us up to the sense of wonder and gratitude that life so generously offers, "Other Places" groups poems from travels away from home.

Ordinary Days

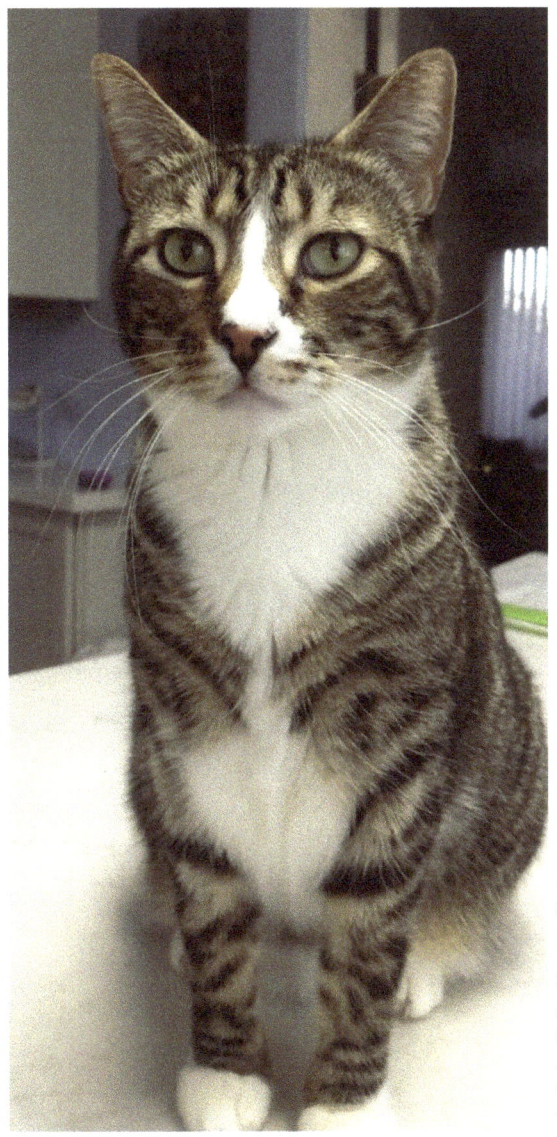

Quincy

photo by Kathy Kramer-Howe

Starbuck's Twenty-Gram Protein Box

Chew the string cheese
till its solid milkiness
tastes like childhood.

Crack and pulverize
the small carrot bones
into carotene mush.

You crave a Eucharist
from that small plastic box.
Absolution is needed.

May the zucchini wafers
dipped in yogurt sauce
become your body.

May the quarter sandwich
of peanut butter and jelly
become the world's salt,

grain and sweetness,
pardon you for your wasteful
life, for not being there

in Gaza to spoon food
into a child's mouth,
for how we cannot

disagree and still enjoy
each other. May these
twenty grams of grace

be the transformation
that digests the world,
offers it back changed.

The Kestrels Fledge

On a thirty-foot queen palm, American kestrels
raise a family this spring. Once eggs are laid,
she disappears into a crag, he hunts lizards,
mice, even birds. At first and last light,
he stands sentinel-like, creamy breast
glowing east at dawn, west at end of day.

Friday, two juveniles emerge lurching
and peering from their high platform,
then two more. They stagger about, stretch
stubby wings, fluff and curry pale coats.
When a parent touches down to drop
a mouse, they plunge at it, squealing.

Late this morning one lifts off (it looks
like falling). The wings catch and hold.
By tomorrow, all four will leap into
destiny's care. Could there be finer
employment than replenishing the earth
with tiny falcons, with their rust and blue
warrior paint, downy pantaloons,
ferrety, implacable eyes?

They contemplate each dawn, each dusk
as if their DNA remembers the Fifth Day,
emerging from Creation's fingers
and being tossed into a lit world.

Trespassing as Fine Art

At a neighbor's rosemary hedge,
I stoop and snip six branches,
cautiously. Bees hum among
hundreds of flowers. My pocket
smells bracing, pungent, like
the pork and polenta I will season.

I harvest three lemons from another
neighbor's tree, perfect agates
on dark branches. I don't ask
for permission, so many already
cratered and bruised on the ground.

Before home, I trespass again
to greet a rose, golden geode
in my cupped hands, thrilling
as a ship's sunstruck billows
might appear to a castaway,
the scent more seductive
than a perfumed neck.
She won't last. I leave her there.

Hawks

Yesterday, I woke
to the knife cries of hawks
hurling their fierce demand
at the still air.

There were three,
soldier-stiff
on tops of poles,
heads swiveling
unnaturally.

Nothing stirred.
The cat watched near cover,
and I, breathless as prey,
senses and energies armed,
yearned for that purity:

I am!
I am here and now!
Give me, world,
give me what I need.

Hot Latte, Sprinkle of Lavender

Waiting at the trendy coffee shop to hear
my name scrawled on a honey lavender latte.
I look around: crumpled patches of sun
on Camelback Mountain, other people
seated on the patio. Bent like fortune cookies,
each one stares into a laptop's open, glowing
envelope, flipping through its messages.
Unseen by them, I notice the expensive frayed
jeans, clear plastic backless heels, carefully
knotted scarf, dog ignored under the table,
unexpectedly think of the German movie
Wings of Desire, when angels in gray overcoats,
invisible to those around them, hover close,
sense the loneliness, elation, despair
of humans, whisper urgently when one
gets too close to jumping. I want to be
one of those angels, perhaps eternally sipping
my steaming latte, to come close behind each
one of those. I want to trace my index finger
gently from the base of their spines
to their occipital bones until they uncurl
like those time-lapse images of seedlings,
blink, wonder where they've been.

Bella Knew She Was Borrowed

Bella knew she was borrowed
but didn't care. I had the leash
and her owner's okay.
"Best duck retriever I ever had,"
he smiled, "in her day."
She tugged me politely
for a block or two
until I unhooked her.
I know the rules, said her backward
glance. *You can trust me.*

We passed bushes and patches
of winter grass
and U-shaped driveways
she considered and rejected.
She greeted other walkers
by leaning on their legs.

Then Bella found a filthy
torn tennis ball
and transformed.
Dancing backwards before me
she riveted her eyes on the ball.
Her haunches shook violently.
Her every fiber demanded
to retrieve that lump of canvas—
in midair, on the run, on the scoot—
and deposit it hungrily
at my feet. Finally, I hid
the soggy scrap under a bush
and called her onward.

To my astonishment,
she shed her infatuation
without a glance
and trotted ahead.

I know how to grasp and claim,
how to worry a thought
into a worn and tattered thing.

I have even felt the passion
I saw in that black Lab,
(although her intensity shook
her like a kind of terror).

It is the letting go
that eludes me—
how to drop
at the side of the path
the thing I most adore,
how to turn
with a clean expectation
and step
into the freefall
of the moment.

Wake-Up Call

Slumber holds me
in a soft-sided clutch
of smoky satin.
Waking pushes open
its flap weighted
with jewels.

The ceiling fan drops
coils of cool air
like spiral peelings
from a pear.
Ladders of grey light
press against
the glass door.

Lying here, I am not
yet anywhere–
conscious of being
yet not of being me.

Then life settles
the question
with its insistent hungers.

A Colombian Woman Makes Hot Chocolate in Phoenix

An ingot of mottled cacao clangs
against the bottom of the pot, into
which she pours several cups of almond
milk, hooks on a metal tea egg filled
with star anise (like a dried spider,
her husband always says,) allspice
berries from Pimento trees, and cloves,
then warms it over low flame.

Around the kitchen island, we watch
the pot, talk, slow each other down.
Best if it comes to three or four boils,
she says, but we will just have one. Soon,
she adds a teaspoon of vanilla, a cinnamon
stick, orange skin grated fine as pine pollen.
We check the clock, watch the pot.

She spins the molinillo against one steady
hand to froth the mixture, bring it to one
slow boil. Someone remarks that
an immersion blender would be faster.

Then the honey and cayenne levels are tested.
Slowly she calibrates the sweetness
and heat, passes spoons to taste, fills mugs
for each of us when it is just right.

Exactly eight servings empty the pot.
In silence, we sip the thick, complex
elixir, its chemistry rehearsed
over generations to inundate the senses
and remind us that there are things
more worthwhile saving than time.

Cat Quincy's Magnificent Sniffer

There's a lot of chopping for chicken soup
and Quincy wants to examine every
nubbin, nugget and scrap.

He perches like a big, furry Hershey's Kiss
on the stool, and with funnel ears
and quivering muzzle follows projectiles flying
from board to trash: flayed carrot skin,
earthy Portobello stumps, green onion roots
like many-fingered barnacles. I slide chopped
mounds into broth, add chicken, acrid oregano.

Quincy knows each thing by scent and sound,
knows when a morsel misses the bin.
With every pivot, I lean, inhale the scent
between his ears, like a baby's flannel,
exhale warm breath into his small, rust-colored
nose shaped like a vase with wings
or tiny ovaries or a valentine, fourteen times
more enchanted than I by the universe of smells.

In Front of the Meat Display

Is anything decent on sale—he likes sales—
anything I can cook enough of for days?

I picture chicken in a pan four ways,
beans and chard, zucchini and potatoes,

artichokes with rice. I'd need rice.
Or pasta? Do I have potatoes?

As captive and cold as the meat below,
I stand still, scan, and strategize

as if the items I select could
settle the Middle East, as if

I might have to return the money
for the Nobel Prize for Peace

if I don't get our dinner on the table
by the end of the evening news.

Everyday Miracles

At Starbucks, I have them
print **Nina** on the label
of my toasted coconut
iced Grande cold brew.

I see on her paper mug
that the young woman
beside me on the patio
is called **Amanda.**

She is reading a real book,
pink and yellow markers
at hand. She glances up,
tosses me a smile.

Led out of the animal hospital
next door, a retriever grins
and dances on her leash:
This is more like it!!

Across the asphalt lot,
scent of sizzling garlic.
Red neon sign entices me
to visit Ristorante L'Amoré.

O Starbucks, **Amanda,**
L'Amoré, dogs—everywhere
life is showering us
with everyday miracles.

For Success in Aging

Years ago, if you boated along the canals
of France, the lock keepers were elderly
widows of veterans. A slow process

waiting for sluices to lower or raise
the pound level so the gate behind
or in front of you could close.

Then stalled between dank, mossy walls,
wait for the container to fill or drain. Slow
waiting, slow gates creaking open again.

The sociable, hardy widows now gone,
their huts put to new use, mechanical
aids installed. Let us gather some friends,

rent a barge, drink wine, dawdle
along the placid Saône or Canal du Midi.
We can clamber out to operate the locks,

wait for the river to spill and gush out and in
releasing the boat to the next meandering horizon
where, loose and alive, we take in the passing shore.

Forgetfulness

Lynn at Solomon Islands Harbor

Lynn Marsh Hill
April 7, 1942 - December 4, 2024

Breezy Point, Maryland

Six-thirty and body sinks into the bed,
thoughts bob on the surface. I give up
on sleep, grip my coffee mug like a buoy,
step in dark onto the asphalt driveway,
leaves glued by dew and passing rain,
morning leaden as the nearby bay.

Despite the pandemic, I came
for my sister to shoulder a bit
of her closing-in life, daily small
losses in smaller spaces—glasses,
notes to self, keys, rotting sack
of groceries, three months of mail.
I try not to shame her forgetfulness.

Today I will sort out her fridge, hook
on an emergency lockbox, change
sheets in her dark box of a bedroom.

Close beside me, Carolina wren, first
brave bird of dawn, calls.

Chesapeake Nightfall

I spend the afternoon deep in
her fridge soaking, scraping, pitching
sealed packets of smoked salmon
six years old, four bottles of gourmet
red wine vinegar, cheeses gone from
aged to ancient. Double-bag garbage,
salvage cardboard, empty and wash
dozens of prepared meal containers
never opened. Lug the mess to
Plum Point Transfer Center.

At twilight, we sit in her Prius
at Breezy Point Beach,
gaze at the lamina of sand,
steel-washed bay, delicately
scrolling pastel clouds.

Six black pilings stitch sky to land.
From here we can't see the tideline,
a massacre of horseshoe crabs,
some clenched like a child's fist.

At the Eye Doctor

The young tech who measures
my sister's vision shouts her questions:
"Now with glasses on—now off,
no, now on–no, Ma'am, off!"

Laboring to breathe, my sister drops
her surgical mask below her nose.
"Mask up, mask up, Ma'am.
Head still–look at this finger!"

We move to other rooms, scary
machines, frowning technicians.

My sister knows she is failing the tests.
Does anyone pass? The waiting room
chairs are full of deficiencies:
cataracts, glaucoma, astigmatism.

Finally, the ophthalmologist
and her assistant enter our little room.
No one acknowledges me, seated
just behind their backs.

My sister fails the eyedrops test,
can't recall the bottle lid color.

She is derelict in ocular care.
There will be a make-up test
in two months. At check-out,
the gentle-voiced receptionist

looks into my sister's blinded pupils,
offers a flat packet of dark glasses.

A Shrine in Paradise, Prince Frederick

The twenty steps from car to Paradise
Nail & Spa leave her breathless, wounded
almost, collapsed on nearest chair before she
makes her slow way to the foot-bath recliner.

Below the check-out counter, the ancestor altar
is red and gold, bowls of rice, foil-wrapped coins,
round-bellied bearded statuettes with venerable
smiles, peaches, ceramic Lucky Cat whose bobble

paw waves forward-back, forward-back. If
she'd noticed it, my sister might have smiled,
forgotten it within a minute. I pay the bill,
help her back to the rented car, fingernails,

tips of toes "Wish You Were Here" scarlet.
As we drive back to assisted living, I wish
I'd left a few coins for the ghosts, kept them happy,
prayed for memory, for mercy, for ease of breath.

Saint Patrick's Day

On Saint Patrick's Day, I return
to North Beach at dusk after freighting
my sister's needs all day.

This is a night for barhopping
and shedding green glitter.
I order takeout and carry my wine
to the sidewalk. People amble
back and forth across the street
between the only two bars in town.

I raise my plastic goblet to beer-laced
embraces, slackened couples laughing.

A hired trio lugs amplifiers and fiddle case
from the Guinness place, gig over.
The singer, in stilettos and green-sequined
mini dress, carefully navigates the steps down.

With my sack of crabcakes growing cold,
I follow her up the street toward
my rented cottage, the waiting bed.

At the end of the block, the Chesapeake
lies gray, inert like a full stop.

Birthday Dinner

On the occasion of your eightieth birthday,
we three sisters linger over an evening
meal on Solomon's Island. Our conjoined
lifetimes create a chalice, and you emerge
as I remember you in your twenties—
the same shy, brilliant smile.

With snatches of French, you recall
Paris before the rest of us arrived.
We spotted you in the street, wet hair
and flip-flops, after your hammam bath.

Later in New York during the drinking,
you were a junior editor at William Morris
(recommended "Papillon," in French,
for publication, a small triumph of taste).

For two hours in the café, you are you.
But on the short drive home, you say
you've been forgetting things like
how to go to bed. You ask, "How can I
go to bed when there is no bedroom?"
Something you have done over twenty-nine
thousand times is fading.
What will go next?

Bearded Irises in North Beach

There are bearded irises
beside the rental porch rail—
tissue froths of lavender and gold.

A cloud-high canopy
tints the air green.
Trees have leafed lavishly.

I have rented vacation cottages
in this bayside village
in cool, clammy autumns,

stark winters, a rare blizzard,
other burgeoning springs.
Today, I am losing track.

Does this all happen without
me? Am I the continuity
even as my sister enters

an untethered present?
Last spring's blossoms
are mulch and worms.

Yet, here I am again, and here
is an acclamation of irises,
heart-stopping in showy gowns.

They try to tell me something
about offering oneself to life,
but I can only hear their beauty.

Empty Nest

I had rummaged often through your kitchen drawers.
There were no matches. Caregivers warming your
        food
had no need for flame. You never ventured from sofa
to stove. How did you find the box? Yet, that very day

caregivers saw you strike match to rolled paper,
raise it toward canula oxygen flow, ending
your time in independent living. "I don't know
why I did it," you said, "but I knew." Afterwards,

when you were safe in a nursing home room,
when your treasures were packed or given away,
your old dog was moved to another state,
and night calls from panicked staff had ended,

why did my heart feel so empty and haunted
as if fired from a job that I never wanted?

Binary

It's our last supper before I leave again.
You've just devoured two bacon-wrapped
scallops from The Lighthouse when you
lift your eyes to mine and something shifts.

It's like when our father was dying. His
blue eyes opened to me and his spirit
said, right into my mind, *I'm going now.*

You swell up, double over coughing
so hard I run for the nurse. It shakes you,
plunders, like an animal desperate to escape.

Stark as a switch, I see you here/gone,
here, slumped over your frail chest. Gone.
We lay you in bed, and tomorrow, you wake up.
But now I have seen it, how easy the grim toggle.

Searching for Jug Bay Sanctuary

I drive you into the rolling
farmland of southeast Maryland,
miles of white fences, cartoon barns,
crayon colors: tree, sun, horse.

Far from anything we recognize,
I turn onto a back road with a sign:
Jug Bay This Way. In deep woods,
I stop the car, and side-by-side we sit.

The silence is lush and thick. Enrapt,
content, you listen as few people
listen to a language we both recall,
one that cannot be lost or taken away.

As toddlers, we sat on a beach,
looked up at a camera, our fingers
plunged in something cool and heavy.
Behind us the sea rocked and hushed.

Harbor

for Lynn in memoriam

We spent twenty minutes with her body,
only her head visible in the funeral drapery.
They had forced her mouth to close.
I knew her, pressed palms to her cold,
rigid face, wept. Afterwards,
we visit the places and watery expanses
our older sister loved.

At Anne Marie Garden's annual
holiday craft fair, my sister Sally and I
purchase two small paintings of local
boats floating at anchor.

From the boardwalk at North Beach,
its Christmas arches shuddering in wind,
we each release a handful of beach sand
into the Chesapeake, contemplate
its gray, choppy candor, everything
wordless, possible.

Back home, I gaze into my painting,
the white hull and gunwales of a fishing boat
glowing at dawn in Solomons Harbor.
What draws my eye are rippling reflections
of what I can't see, what is just outside the frame.

Other Places

Touching Mainos

Massachusetts in May

I

Spring winds, seasonal heralds,
excite the pines like heaving bodices.
I rake black humus from fern beds, cart
goo into the woods. A flock of early robins
scatters across the lawn. They tread
slowly, hop onto a breeze, then pace
like monks pondering ultimate matters.

II

I cannot pass the din on Chestnut Hill Road
without stopping beside soggy vernal ground.
Manic drone, like out-of-tune accordions,
is peppered by a deeper fusillade.
"That's peepers," drawls the farmer,
"and that there's croakers." All
day and night, a gay boggy squall.

Not Raindrops

You would swear
it was raining.
You would swear it.

On the lake, sky is mottled stoneware,
shore an open bolt of green silk.

As far as you can see,
the graphite-smooth surface
is pocked with droplets.

Yet nothing is falling.
Instead, countless tiny water striders
skim the surface.

They push off with back legs, oar
with front ones in jerky whorls,
a galaxy of interlapping circles.

The spell of water
can capture the sky,
make it stone, or

turn its liquid skin
into silent rain.

York Beach, Maine

compact
crescent so flat
I could walk hundreds
of steps toward water with
dry ankles, so finely sifted over
millions of years, sand gleams
like mercury, wet as thickset cement.
At low tide, couples stroll on their shadows,
dogs pick up steam, run full out for a ball, paws
hovering above the beach, tongues loose.
A distant fringe of water chews placidly
on the silt, takes its time, tells that time
is a circular stirring we call years,
wears away black granite shoals,
coastal cottages, human hearts,
memories, this memory,
this wet shining
hour.

Floating, Desolation Canyon, Utah

We are drifting down a jade-green river,
the raft piled high with camping gear.
Our guide, Turner, listlessly rows, tumbles
overboard to cool off, heaves back on, glossy

with water, and that's when the spider bloom
begins, first a few strands caught in his hair,
then loose crochets of silk rising, sun-lit
against dark, primordial cliffs. A perfect breeze

lofts them ever higher, where a falcon flutters,
snacking on spiderlings. An eddy spins us,
and briefly we follow the balloons upstream,
before turning into the lazy flow, while silvery

tangles ascend past narrow canyon walls,
floating on the updraft as far as they will go.

Note:
When small spiders sense electrical fields from the upper atmosphere, or an ideal breeze, they can tiptoe, and from lifted spinnerets extrude several strands of silk, waiting to be snatched up into the air. The phenomenon is called ballooning. Huge collections of sailing spiderlings can travel a few miles or even across oceans to new lands.

At the Tambo Hotel, Johannesburg

The dining room carpet is plush;
wind lashes trees beyond glass
doors, litters the blue-lit pool;

and, with my husband, I eat
nasi goreng sixty years after
my student months on Bali,

now in the land where my first love
was born, a White South African
dissident who fled persecution,

and when I approach the buffet
the twenty-year-old Black waiter
murmurs, "Hello, goo goo," so

I turn and smile up at him, a man
who inhabits his hips when he walks,
his masculinity front and forward,

and old as I am, I return to table,
whole memories newly spliced,
and woman again at my core.

Feeling Mainos

"Through the Eyes of an Elephant"
is the experience I pay for, drive
twenty-five minutes from Victoria Falls

to an elephant sanctuary where a herd
of elephants is cared for in nature.
Mainos is my elephant, one-tusked

twenty-seven-year-old bull on birth control.
With one hand, I pack his eager
nostrils with molasses and oat cubes,

and with the other, stroke his trunk,
a rough, corrugated tube of muscle,
huge restless nozzle sprouting

hairs like heavy-gauge wire.
The handler bungs more treats
into his nose which closes like a fist,

curls, blows the cargo into his mouth,
sniffs for the bag, reaches for more,
understands how much I want him.

Punta Moreno Landing, Galápagos

Our chartered catamaran bucks,
pitches, shudders all night
to reach the western shore
of Isla Isabela.

We awake rocking gently
off a barren island, volcanic calderas
on flattened horizon. Legs rubbery,
we file onto lava fields as jagged
as petrified wind-buckled waves.

Like space explorers beamed down,
we lurch forward. There is nothing
here but lizards, lava cactus, fish
stranded in isolated lagoons, visiting
pelicans and flamingos. In the crawl
toward complexity, we won't belong
for tens of millions of years.

We peer about, grow silent,
wait for our bearings.

Ocean Inside

From behind my eyes to sand-burnished feet,
there is just ocean.

Hands at my sides, propelled by fins,
I peer through shoals of flashing fish,
silver over blue over yellow.
They stream like bubbles
from fissures in stone and coral
or rock placidly in the current.

Shocking in their neon costumes,
king angelfish rasp on lava crusts.

A young seal spirals toward me,
gazes with curious eyes,
glides beneath, reappears, tempts
me, in my warm blood, to follow.

Her shell a mossy olive,
green turtle munches algae
and ignores me, spread-eagled
above like a cloud.

O, Galápagos, your saltiness
turns my heart into an ocean.

Pine Woods Triptych, Flagstaff

I

Ravens are watchdogs of the woods.
Four of them rise into positions
above me, bark nonstop with that
iron-against-washboard rasp
until I leave their invisible rooms,
then all together stop, open black
wings, circle the boundary, drop.

II

I close my eyes to a moving weave
of trees. They glide by each other
in silence, a company of columns,
smooth, bronze, topped with green.
Now I stand tap-rooted like wood
while they slide over forest floor.
I'd dance among them if I could.

III

I want to know them by name:
Arizona Lupine, Woolly Mullein,
Indian Paintbrush, Skyrocket.
In clearings edged with feathered grass,
they live together in sunny soil.
I pull a pale stem from a blade,
suck sweet green like new olive oil.

Two White-Tailed Deer Near an Abbey

On the pitted, rock-strewn road from
the monastery, I walk late in the day.
Ahead, two white-tailed deer, a mother
and yearling, nibble wintry straw.

The doe sees me, freezes. I stop
on the heels of my companion shadow.
We wait motionless long enough
for vesper bells to ring on the hill.

Then she moves. The air ripples.
Out of stillness steps a glorious deer
as if emerging from a cleft
between being and oblivion.

So many living things, outlines
erased, voices stilled, will never
more appear through that portal.
But what these deer know today

is that this is sanctuary ground.
I come to them from silence.
At the edge of this dormant field
there is still some green grass.

We Made It From . . .

We made it from fireflies in Mason jars
winking hard at their reflections,
tossed up to the stars.

We made it from aerosol of skin
under full sun and the boat crawling
ahead of the wind.

We added that spacious moment
when, in Eastern woods bright with
new snow, we stopped, breathing clouds.

We made it from your eyes meeting mine,
drank it in a land before time, spilled
it on sun-scorched painted shards.

Acknowledgements

I am grateful for the people who surround me with friendship and intimacy. I know who they are as soon as I imagine my life without them in it. My local Circle of Writers, COW, poetry group helped to refine many of these poems.

My husband and life-partner, Rick, ponders things ranging from popular lyrics to the velocity of the cosmos. Together we keep curiosity and wonder alive.

I am indebted to my publisher, Marcia Gagliardi, who has believed in and supported my voice, giving it a presence in published form. Thank you.

Without a spiritual grounding, I doubt I would have written any of the poems in *Searching for Jug Bay Sanctuary*. For me, spiritual grounding is a daily practice of Centering Prayer, supported by Contemplative Outreach, Ltd.

Kathy Kramer-Howe

About the Author

    Kathy Kramer-Howe is a retired hospice social worker and bereavement counselor. That career, begun in her mid fifties, became her true vocation. She has written prose and poetry most of her life but began focusing on the craft of poetry a few years ago when she joined a circle of writers and began attending workshops and study groups.

    Kathy and her husband, Rick, live in the Sonoran Desert of southern Arizona and return often to Orange, Massachusetts, where the Howe family has lived for generations. Her family maintains a hundred-year-old cottage on Lake Mattawa.

    *Searching for Jug Bay Sanctuary i*s her second book of poetry. The first is *Lake Mattawa 2020: a pandemic, a small cemetery, and a month alone.*

Colophon

Text and captions in *Searching for Jug Bay Sanctuary* are set in Bookmania, designed in 2011 by Mark Simonson. Bookmania combines the elegance of the original Bookman Oldstyle, 1901, with the swashy exuberance of the Bookmans of the 1960s, according to Simonson.

Bookmania includes more than 680 swash characters, each a decorative letter with an extended stroke, serif, or terminal. Unlike some Bookman revivals, it retains the original classic sloped roman for the italic.

Titles and subtitiles in *Searching for Jug Bay Sanctuary* are set in Tahoma, a humanist sans-serif typeface that Matthew Carter designed for Microsoft Corporation. Microsoft first distributed it as a computer font with Office 97.

While similar to Verdana, Tahoma has a narrower body, smaller counters, much tighter letter spacing, and a more complete Unicode character set. Carter first designed Tahoma as a bitmap font, then wrapped TrueType outlines around those bitmaps. Carter based the bold weight on a double pixel width, rendering it closer to a heavy or black weight.

Great Blue Heron
watercolor on paper by Kathy Kramer-Howe

www.ingramcontent.com/pod-product-compliance
Lightning Source LLC
Chambersburg PA
CBHW040312050426
42451CB00020B/3492